Table Of Contents

Chapter 1: Understanding Seasonal Affective Disorder (SAD) 1
Chapter 2: The Role of Generative AI in Mental Health 1
Chapter 3: AI-Powered Mood Tracking Apps for SAD 1
Chapter 4: Virtual Reality Environments for Seasonal Light Therapy 1
Chapter 5: Personalized AI Therapy Chatbots for SAD Support 1
Chapter 6: Generative AI for Creating Seasonal Wellness Plans 1
Chapter 7: AI-Driven Community Support Platforms for SAD Awareness 1
Chapter 8: Integrating Generative AI in Traditional Mental Health Practices 1
Chapter 9: Challenges and Limitations of AI in Addressing SAD 1
Chapter 10: Conclusion and Future Perspectives 1
Preface 1

Preface

Generative AI, Gen AI. Here to support all and not focused on popular media grabbing popularity. To day Kuldeepuk Kohli talks about Seasonal affective disorder (SAD) and how Gen AI is making life better for those who suffer from SAD. Currently there is no charity worldwide focused on Seasonal affective disorder (SAD). There are organisations that support but they also support other conditions such as Campaign Against Living Miserably (CALM) or Rethink. None are focused on SAD. The NHS UK estimate that around 2 million people in the UK and 12 million people across northern Europe experience SAD every year. Seasonal affective disorder (SAD) is a type of depression that comes and goes in a seasonal pattern. SAD is sometimes known as "winter depression" because the symptoms are usually more apparent and more severe during the winter. Some people with SAD may have symptoms during the summer. Symptoms of SAD vary from person to person. You may not experience a whole range of symptoms, and they may come in waves as the weather continues to progressively change. Symptoms include Persistent low mood, Low interest in socialising, Guilt, Feeling more stressed than usual, Lowered libido, Concentration issues, Irritation and short temper, Disinterest in enjoyable things and activities, Feelings of despair and worthlessness amongst other symptoms. Gen AI is here to help. Predicting Emotional States Using Behavioural Markers Derived from Passively Sensed Data by using Gen AI. In a recent study by California Correctional Health Care Services. Their Objective: Aims to present a Gen AI approach for emotional state prediction that uses passively collected data from mobile phones and wearable devices and self-reported emotions. The proposed methods cope with high-dimensional and heterogeneous time-series data with a large percentage of missing observations. The Method used for the research. Passively sensed behaviour and self-reported emotional state data from a cohort of 943 individuals (outpatients recruited from community clinics) were available for analysis by Gen AI. All patients had at least 30 days' worth of naturally occurring behaviour observations, including information about physical activity, geolocation, sleep, and smartphone app use. These regularly sampled but frequently missing and heterogeneous time series were analysed by Gen AI with the following probabilistic latent variable models for data averaging and feature extraction: mixture model (MM) and hidden Markov model (HMM). The extracted features were then combined with a classifier to predict emotional state. A variety of Gen AI learning methods and recurrent neural networks were compared. Finally, a personalized Bayesian model was proposed to improve performance by considering the individual differences in the data and applying a different classifier bias term for each patient. The results were clear.

Probabilistic generative models generated by Gen AI proved to be good pre-processing and feature extractor tools for data with large percentages of missing observations. Models that considered the posterior probabilities of the MM and HMM latent states outperformed those that did not by more than 63%, suggesting that the underlying behavioural patterns identified were meaningful for individuals' overall emotional state. The best performing generalized models achieved a 0.81 area under the curve of the receiver operating characteristic and 0.71 area under the precision-recall curve when predicting self-reported emotional valence from behaviour in held-out test data. Moreover, the proposed personalized models demonstrated that accounting for individual differences through a simple hierarchical model can substantially improve emotional state prediction performance without relying on previous days' data. Kuldeepuk Kohli Bringing the benefits of generative AI , Gen AI to make life better for all even with lesser supported conditions such as Seasonal affective disorder (SAD) which is relevant to the season we now enter in the winter months. Thanks for watching.

Chapter 1: Understanding Seasonal Affective Disorder (SAD)

Definition and Symptoms of SAD

Seasonal Affective Disorder (SAD) is a type of depression that typically occurs during specific seasons, most commonly in the fall and winter when daylight hours are shorter. It is characterized by a persistent low mood, lack of energy, and a general sense of hopelessness. The condition is believed to be triggered by changes in light exposure, which can affect the body's internal clock and alter the levels of chemicals such as serotonin and melatonin. While many people may experience mild seasonal mood changes, those with SAD face more severe symptoms that can significantly impact their daily lives.

Symptoms of SAD can vary widely among individuals but often include feelings of sadness, anxiety, and irritability. Individuals may also experience changes in sleep patterns, such as oversleeping or insomnia, alongside alterations in appetite, which can lead to weight gain or loss. Fatigue is another common symptom, making it difficult for individuals to engage in everyday activities. Cognitive difficulties, including problems with concentration and decision-making, are also prevalent, contributing to a decreased quality of life.

In the UK alone, approximately two million people are affected by SAD, while the figure rises to about 12 million across Northern Europe. The geographical prevalence of SAD suggests a connection to light exposure, with those living in regions with long winters and limited sunlight being at higher risk. This disorder can affect individuals of any age, but it often emerges during late adolescence or early adulthood. Understanding the demographics and psychological implications of SAD is crucial for developing effective prevention and treatment strategies.

Generative AI technologies are emerging as powerful tools to support individuals dealing with SAD. AI-powered mood tracking apps can help users monitor their emotional states over time, identifying patterns and triggers associated with their symptoms. These applications can provide insights into how seasonal changes affect mood, allowing for proactive management and timely interventions. Additionally, virtual reality environments designed for seasonal light therapy can simulate natural sunlight, helping to alleviate symptoms by enhancing mood and energy levels through exposure to bright light.

Personalized AI therapy chatbots and AI-driven community support platforms offer innovative approaches to SAD awareness and treatment. These tools can provide immediate support and resources tailored to individual needs, ensuring that users receive relevant guidance and encouragement throughout their seasonal challenges. Generative AI can also assist in creating customized seasonal wellness plans that incorporate lifestyle changes, therapeutic practices, and community engagement, fostering resilience and promoting overall well-being during difficult months.

Prevalence and Impact on Society

Seasonal Affective Disorder (SAD) is a prevalent mental health condition that affects millions of individuals each year, particularly in regions with long winters and limited sunlight. In the UK alone, approximately 2 million people experience symptoms of SAD annually, while around 12 million individuals are affected across northern Europe. The condition typically manifests during the fall and winter months, leading to feelings of depression, lethargy, and social withdrawal. Understanding the scope of SAD is vital for healthcare professionals and mental health practitioners, as it emphasizes the need for effective interventions and the potential role of generative AI technologies in addressing this widespread issue.

The impact of SAD extends beyond individual experiences, influencing societal well-being and productivity. Individuals suffering from SAD may struggle to maintain their daily responsibilities, which can result in increased absenteeism in workplaces and educational settings. This not only affects the individuals but also places a burden on families, communities, and the economy as a whole. The repercussions of untreated SAD can lead to more severe mental health issues, further complicating treatment efforts and resource allocation within the healthcare system. Addressing this condition effectively is crucial for fostering a healthier, more productive society.

Emerging technologies, particularly generative AI, offer promising avenues for supporting individuals with SAD. AI-powered mood tracking apps can help users monitor their emotional states and identify patterns related to their symptoms. By collecting data over time, these applications can provide personalized insights that empower users to manage their condition proactively. Furthermore, such tools can facilitate early intervention by alerting individuals to significant changes in their mood, potentially guiding them toward appropriate professional support or self-care strategies.

Virtual reality environments have also emerged as an innovative approach to seasonal light therapy. By simulating natural sunlight exposure, these immersive experiences can alleviate symptoms of SAD for users who may have limited access to sunlight during the darker months. The effectiveness of this therapy can be further enhanced through AI algorithms that adapt the virtual environment based on user preferences and responses, creating a tailored therapeutic experience. This personalized approach to light therapy underscores the potential of generative AI in crafting effective solutions for mental health challenges.

In addition to mood tracking and light therapy, generative AI can play a crucial role in the development of personalized wellness plans for individuals with SAD. By analyzing user data, including lifestyle habits and symptom patterns, AI-driven systems can generate customized strategies that promote seasonal well-being. Moreover, AI-driven community support platforms can foster awareness and connection among individuals experiencing SAD, reducing the stigma associated with mental health conditions. These platforms can also serve as valuable resources for education and shared experiences, creating a supportive network that enhances overall mental health in society.

The Science Behind Seasonal Mood Changes

The phenomenon of seasonal mood changes is deeply rooted in biological, psychological, and environmental factors. Seasonal

Affective Disorder (SAD) affects millions of individuals, particularly in regions with limited sunlight during the winter months. Research indicates that fluctuations in daylight exposure can disrupt circadian rhythms and melatonin production, leading to mood disturbances. The brain's neurotransmitters, such as serotonin, also play a critical role in regulating mood, with decreased sunlight exposure potentially causing a dip in serotonin levels. Understanding the science behind these changes is essential for developing effective interventions, including those powered by generative AI.

Generative AI has emerged as a promising tool in addressing the challenges associated with SAD. AI-powered mood tracking applications can monitor emotional states and patterns over time, providing users with insights into their mood fluctuations related to seasonal changes. By analyzing data such as sleep patterns, activity levels, and environmental factors, these applications can offer personalized recommendations for improving mental health. This approach allows individuals to take proactive steps in managing their mood and can serve as a valuable supplement to traditional therapeutic methods.

Virtual reality (VR) environments have shown potential in mimicking natural light exposure, which is crucial for individuals suffering from SAD. By immersing users in bright, sunny environments, VR can stimulate the brain's response to light, thereby alleviating some symptoms of depression associated with shorter daylight hours. This innovative approach not only provides immediate relief but also encourages individuals to engage in therapeutic activities that might otherwise seem unappealing during the darker months. The integration of VR with AI can further enhance these experiences by personalizing them based on the individual's preferences and mood responses.

Personalized AI therapy chatbots are another innovative solution for those experiencing SAD. These chatbots can provide immediate support and coping strategies tailored to an individual's specific situation. By using natural language processing and machine learning, these AI-driven platforms can adapt their responses based on user interactions, creating a more engaging and supportive experience. This technology can supplement traditional therapy by providing additional resources and support when access to mental health professionals may be limited, especially during peak seasons of SAD.

Finally, AI-driven community support platforms can play a vital role in raising awareness and fostering connections among individuals affected by SAD. These platforms can facilitate discussions, share personal experiences, and provide educational resources about seasonal mood disorders. By leveraging generative AI to analyze community interactions, these platforms can identify trends and tailor content to better meet the needs of users. This collaborative approach not only enhances individual well-being but also builds a sense of community, which is essential for combating the isolation often felt during darker months.

Chapter 2: The Role of Generative AI in Mental Health

Overview of Generative AI Technologies

Generative AI technologies represent a significant advancement in the intersection of artificial intelligence and mental health support, particularly for those affected by Seasonal Affective Disorder (SAD). This condition, which impacts millions of individuals in the UK and Northern Europe each year, is characterized by a pattern of depression that occurs at specific times of the year, typically in the winter months when natural light is scarce. The development of generative AI tools offers innovative solutions that can help alleviate the symptoms of SAD by providing accessible support, personalized interventions, and community engagement.

AI-powered mood tracking applications are one of the most promising innovations in the realm of mental health. These applications utilize generative AI to analyze user data, such as mood patterns, sleep quality, and daily activities, to deliver personalized insights and recommendations. By continuously learning from the user's behavior, these applications can offer timely prompts and interventions that encourage healthier habits and coping strategies. For individuals suffering from SAD, this proactive approach can lead to improved awareness of their mental state and foster a greater sense of control over their well-being.

Virtual reality (VR) environments have emerged as a powerful tool for seasonal light therapy, which is a common treatment for SAD. Generative AI can enhance these VR experiences by creating immersive environments that simulate bright, sunny days, even in the depths of winter. Users can engage with these virtual settings to experience the therapeutic effects of light exposure in a controlled manner. Furthermore, the adaptability of these environments means that they can be tailored to individual preferences, allowing for a more personalized therapeutic experience that resonates with each user's unique needs.

Personalized AI therapy chatbots have also gained traction as a support mechanism for individuals dealing with SAD. These chatbots utilize generative AI to provide conversational support, offering users an accessible platform to express their feelings and receive immediate feedback. By drawing on a vast database of mental health resources and techniques, these chatbots can guide users through cognitive-behavioral exercises, mindfulness practices, and coping strategies tailored to their specific symptoms. The anonymity and convenience of chatbot interactions can reduce barriers to seeking help, making mental health support more reachable for those reluctant to engage in traditional therapy.

Lastly, generative AI is instrumental in the development of community support platforms that raise awareness about SAD and facilitate connections among individuals facing similar challenges. These platforms can leverage AI to analyze community needs, curate relevant resources, and foster discussions that promote understanding and empathy. By creating a supportive online environment, generative AI can empower individuals with SAD to share their experiences, seek advice, and build social connections, thereby combating the isolation often felt during the darker months. Through these varied applications, generative AI technologies hold the potential to transform how we approach seasonal well-being and support for those affected by SAD.

Applications of AI in Mental Health Care

The integration of artificial intelligence in mental health care has opened up innovative avenues for addressing conditions like Seasonal Affective Disorder (SAD). This disorder affects millions, particularly in northern regions, highlighting the urgent need for effective treatments and support systems. AI technologies are being harnessed to create tailored solutions that not only improve diagnosis and treatment but also help individuals manage their symptoms more effectively. From mood tracking applications to virtual reality environments, AI offers a suite of tools designed to enhance seasonal wellbeing.

AI-powered mood tracking apps are emerging as vital resources for individuals experiencing SAD. These applications utilize algorithms to analyze user data, providing insights into mood patterns and seasonal changes. By prompting users to log their feelings and activities, the apps can identify triggers and suggest interventions. This personalized approach allows users to gain a deeper understanding of their emotional states, empowering them to take proactive steps in managing their mental health. The continuous feedback loop created by these apps can significantly enhance the user's ability to cope with the seasonal fluctuations characteristic of SAD.

Virtual reality environments represent another groundbreaking application of AI in mental health care. These immersive experiences can simulate sunlight exposure, effectively mimicking the natural conditions that many individuals lack during darker months. By utilizing AI to tailor these environments to individual preferences, users can engage in therapeutic light therapy sessions from the comfort of their homes. Research shows that such exposure can alleviate symptoms of SAD, making virtual reality a promising adjunct to traditional treatment methods. This technology not only provides immediate relief but also fosters a sense of engagement and connection with the therapeutic process.

Personalized AI therapy chatbots are transforming the way individuals seek support for SAD. These chatbots can deliver evidence-based therapeutic interventions through conversational interfaces, providing real-time assistance and guidance. By leveraging natural language processing, they can engage users in meaningful dialogue, helping them navigate their feelings and develop coping strategies. The convenience of accessing support anytime and anywhere makes these chatbots particularly appealing for those who may feel isolated due to their condition. They serve as a bridge to mental health resources, enhancing accessibility for individuals who might otherwise hesitate to seek help.

Generative AI also plays a pivotal role in creating seasonal wellness plans tailored to individual needs. By analyzing a person's history, preferences, and specific symptoms of SAD, these systems can generate comprehensive plans that incorporate activities, dietary suggestions, and mindfulness practices. This personalized approach not only aids in symptom management but also promotes overall wellbeing. Furthermore, AI-driven community support platforms are emerging to raise awareness about SAD, fostering a sense of belonging among those affected. These platforms facilitate connections, sharing of experiences, and collective strategies for coping, thereby reducing stigma and encouraging open conversations about mental health.

Ethical Considerations in AI Deployment

Ethical considerations in the deployment of artificial intelligence in healthcare, particularly for individuals suffering from Seasonal Affective Disorder (SAD), are paramount. As generative AI technologies become increasingly integrated into mental health strategies, it is essential to address the ethical implications that arise. This includes ensuring that AI systems are designed and implemented with respect for user privacy, informed consent, and the potential biases that may affect outcomes. The sensitivity of mental health data necessitates robust security measures and transparent policies to protect individuals' information from misuse or unauthorized access.

One of the significant ethical concerns involves the accuracy and reliability of AI-powered mood tracking apps. These applications must be rigorously tested and validated to ensure they provide reliable feedback to users. Misleading or inaccurate data can lead to inappropriate interventions or exacerbate a person's condition. It is also crucial to consider the implications of algorithmic bias, which can occur if the data used to train these AI systems does not represent diverse populations. Such biases can result in unequal access to effective treatments for marginalized groups, thus widening the gap in mental health support.

Virtual reality environments designed for seasonal light therapy present unique ethical challenges as well. While these immersive experiences can significantly improve mood and alleviate SAD symptoms, developers must ensure that these technologies are accessible and affordable for all individuals. Moreover, the potential for over-reliance on virtual environments must be addressed. Users should be encouraged to engage with real-world interactions and activities, as these are vital components of a holistic approach to mental well-being. The ethical deployment of virtual reality also includes considering the potential psychological effects of prolonged use, which should be monitored and managed.

The rise of personalized AI therapy chatbots for SAD support raises questions about the nature of therapeutic relationships. While AI can provide immediate support and resources, it cannot replace the nuanced understanding and empathy that human therapists offer. Ethical considerations must include the boundaries of AI's role in mental health care and the importance of facilitating access to human professionals when necessary. Furthermore, transparency regarding the capabilities and limitations of AI chatbots is essential to prevent users from developing unrealistic expectations about their effectiveness.

Lastly, AI-driven community support platforms for SAD awareness must prioritize inclusivity and ethical engagement. These platforms should foster a sense of belonging and encourage open discussions about mental health, while ensuring that they do not inadvertently stigmatize users. Ethical guidelines should be established to govern the sharing of personal experiences and data within these communities, promoting an environment of support without compromising individual privacy. As generative AI continues to evolve, a commitment to ethical practices will be crucial in ensuring that these technologies enhance, rather than hinder, the well-being of those affected by Seasonal Affective Disorder.

Chapter 3: AI-Powered Mood Tracking Apps for SAD

Features and Functionality of Mood Tracking Apps

Mood tracking apps have become increasingly popular as tools for individuals managing their emotional health, particularly for those experiencing Seasonal Affective Disorder (SAD). These applications typically offer a user-friendly interface that allows users to log their moods regularly, providing visual representations of their emotional changes over time. By encouraging daily reflections, these apps help users identify patterns and triggers associated with their mood fluctuations, which can be particularly beneficial during the darker months when SAD symptoms may intensify.

One notable feature of many mood tracking apps is the ability to integrate with wearable technology and other health applications. This integration allows users to collect a broader range of data, such as sleep patterns, physical activity levels, and sunlight exposure. By analyzing this data in conjunction with mood logs, users can gain deeper insights into how various lifestyle factors contribute to their emotional wellbeing. For individuals with SAD, understanding the interplay between these elements can be crucial for developing effective coping strategies.

AI-powered mood tracking apps often leverage machine learning algorithms to provide personalized feedback and recommendations. These apps can analyze individual mood data and suggest tailored interventions, such as specific light therapy techniques or alerting users to engage in certain activities that have historically improved their mood. This level of customization enhances user engagement and efficacy by addressing unique emotional patterns and lifestyle choices, making the management of SAD symptoms more approachable and effective.

In addition to tracking moods, many apps incorporate features that facilitate community support and connection. Users can engage with peer support groups, share experiences, and access resources related to SAD. This communal aspect can help reduce the feelings of isolation that often accompany the disorder, fostering a sense of belonging. The sharing of personal stories and coping strategies amongst users can further enrich the overall experience, providing additional motivation and encouragement in navigating the challenges of SAD.

Furthermore, advancements in generative AI have opened new avenues for creating personalized seasonal wellness plans. These plans can integrate mood tracking data with established therapeutic approaches, generating actionable strategies tailored to individual needs. By utilizing AI to analyze mood trends and seasonal factors, users can receive guidance on how to optimize their wellbeing throughout the year. Features such as reminders for light therapy sessions, suggestions for outdoor activities during sunny days, or prompts for mindfulness exercises can make a significant difference in managing SAD effectively.

Case Studies of Effective Mood Tracking

Case studies illustrate the transformative potential of mood tracking in managing Seasonal Affective Disorder (SAD) through various innovative approaches. One notable example is the use of AI-powered mood tracking apps that have gained traction among individuals experiencing SAD. These applications allow users to log their daily mood fluctuations alongside environmental factors, such as sunlight exposure and weather conditions. By analyzing this data, the apps can provide personalized feedback and coping strategies tailored to the user's patterns. Reports from users indicate that these insights lead to improved awareness of their emotional states and greater engagement in proactive wellness activities.

Another compelling case study involves the integration of virtual reality environments designed specifically for light therapy. Participants in a controlled study reported significant mood improvements after engaging with virtual simulations that mimic bright, sunny environments. These virtual experiences are particularly beneficial for those unable to access natural sunlight during winter months. The immersive nature of virtual reality helps users feel more connected to their surroundings, and the consistent exposure to simulated sunlight has been shown to alleviate some symptoms of SAD, enhancing overall wellbeing.

Personalized AI therapy chatbots also represent a significant advancement in supporting individuals with SAD. In a pilot program, users interacted with a chatbot that utilized natural language processing to provide real-time emotional support and coping techniques. The chatbot was programmed to recognize signs of seasonal depression through users' language patterns and respond with empathy and tailored advice. Participants reported feeling less isolated and more understood, indicating that AI-driven conversations can complement traditional therapeutic methods and provide immediate assistance during difficult times.

Generative AI is making strides in creating personalized seasonal wellness plans, as demonstrated in a recent study where participants utilized AI to generate customized strategies for managing their mood throughout the year. The generative algorithms took into account individual preferences, seasonal patterns, and past experiences, leading to actionable plans that included exercise regimes, dietary recommendations, and social activities. This proactive approach empowered users to take charge of their mental health, fostering a sense of agency and encouraging healthier lifestyle choices.

AI-driven community support platforms are also enhancing awareness and understanding of SAD among broader populations. One case study highlights a platform that connects individuals experiencing similar challenges, providing a space for sharing experiences, resources, and coping strategies. Users reported feeling a sense of belonging and support that was crucial for their mental health. The platform's integration with AI ensures that users receive relevant content and community interactions tailored to their specific needs, promoting a collective effort to combat the stigma surrounding SAD and encouraging open discussions about seasonal wellbeing.

User Experience and Data Privacy Concerns

User experience (UX) plays a critical role in the effective implementation of generative AI tools aimed at supporting individuals with Seasonal Affective Disorder (SAD). For users who may already be grappling with feelings of isolation and despair, the design and usability of AI-powered applications are paramount. A seamless user experience ensures that these individuals can easily navigate the platforms, access relevant resources, and engage with therapeutic interventions without additional barriers. Intuitive interfaces, clear instructions, and accessible features are essential components that can foster a sense of agency and empowerment in users, ultimately enhancing their overall mental health journey.

However, the integration of data privacy measures within these platforms is equally important. Users of AI-powered mood tracking apps and personalized therapy chatbots often share sensitive information regarding their emotional states, triggers, and personal histories. It is vital that developers prioritize data security and transparency to build trust with their users. Implementing robust encryption protocols, offering clear privacy policies, and allowing users to control their data can alleviate concerns about unauthorized access or misuse. By prioritizing privacy, developers can ensure that users feel safe while engaging with technologies designed to support their seasonal wellbeing.

Moreover, the ethical implications surrounding data usage cannot be overlooked. Users must be informed about how their data will be utilized, particularly in AI-driven community support platforms that may aggregate and analyze user data for broader insights. While data-driven approaches can enhance the effectiveness of SAD awareness initiatives, it is crucial to strike a balance between beneficial analytics and individual privacy rights. Ethical guidelines should be established to govern the collection and use of data, ensuring that users' rights are respected while facilitating advancements in understanding and treating SAD.

Incorporating user feedback into the development process is another vital aspect of enhancing both user experience and data privacy. By actively engaging with users, developers can identify pain points and areas for improvement that may not have been anticipated during the initial design phase. User input can guide the refinement of features, ensuring that the applications not only meet clinical needs but also resonate with the emotional and psychological experiences of users dealing with SAD. This iterative approach fosters a sense of community and collaboration, ultimately leading to more effective and user-friendly solutions.

Finally, as generative AI continues to evolve, it is essential for stakeholders in the health care and mental health sectors to advocate for user-centric designs that prioritize both experience and privacy. Collaboration between technologists, mental health professionals, and users is necessary to create solutions that effectively address the unique challenges faced by individuals with SAD. By fostering an environment of trust, transparency, and responsiveness, we can harness the power of generative AI to illuminate pathways to seasonal wellbeing while respecting the rights and needs of every individual.

Chapter 4: Virtual Reality Environments for Seasonal Light Therapy

Introduction to Virtual Reality Therapy

Virtual Reality Therapy (VRT) is an innovative approach that integrates immersive technology to provide therapeutic experiences for individuals facing various mental health challenges, including Seasonal Affective Disorder (SAD). This technique utilizes virtual environments to simulate natural light exposure and other stimuli that can positively impact mood and emotional well-being. With approximately 2 million individuals in the UK and 12 million across Northern Europe affected by SAD annually, VRT presents a promising avenue for therapeutic intervention in treating this seasonal condition.

The core principle of VRT is to create realistic and engaging environments that can evoke positive emotional responses. By replicating settings associated with warmth, sunlight, and nature, VRT can help mitigate the feelings of depression and lethargy often associated with SAD. The technology allows patients to escape to these virtual worlds, providing a sense of relief and enhancing their overall mood. This method not only addresses the symptoms of SAD but also offers a practical solution for individuals who may find traditional therapies less accessible during peak seasons of their condition.

In conjunction with VRT, generative AI technologies are emerging as vital tools for enhancing the efficacy of treatment. AI-powered mood tracking apps can monitor individuals' emotional states and provide insights into their specific triggers and patterns related to SAD. This data can inform personalized therapeutic interventions delivered through VR environments, making the treatment more effective. By leveraging the power of AI, practitioners can better understand their patients' needs and tailor virtual experiences to optimize therapeutic outcomes.

Another significant advancement in this field is the use of personalized AI therapy chatbots. These chatbots can provide support and resources to individuals experiencing SAD, offering immediate assistance and guidance when human therapists may not be available. By integrating these chatbots with VRT, users can engage in a comprehensive therapeutic experience that combines emotional support with immersive virtual environments. This dual approach can foster a more supportive and responsive treatment framework for those grappling with seasonal mood fluctuations.

As awareness of SAD continues to grow, the development of AI-driven community support platforms is becoming increasingly important. These platforms can facilitate connections among individuals experiencing similar challenges, fostering a sense of community and mutual support. By combining these platforms with virtual reality therapy, individuals can share their experiences and coping strategies while also participating in guided virtual sessions designed to uplift their spirits. Together, these innovations represent a significant step forward in the treatment of Seasonal Affective Disorder, harnessing the potential of technology to enhance mental health care.

Benefits of VR for SAD Treatment

The increasing prevalence of Seasonal Affective Disorder (SAD) has prompted the exploration of innovative treatment options, and Virtual Reality (VR) technology has emerged as a promising tool in this realm. VR offers immersive experiences that can simulate natural environments, effectively addressing the environmental triggers of SAD. By providing users with access to bright, engaging virtual landscapes, VR can help mitigate the feelings of lethargy and sadness that often accompany this condition, making it a valuable adjunct to traditional treatments.

One significant benefit of VR in SAD treatment is its potential for light therapy. Individuals suffering from SAD typically experience a lack of sunlight during the darker months, which can impact their mood and energy levels. VR environments can be designed to replicate sunny, bright settings, allowing users to experience the positive effects of light exposure without having to be outdoors. This approach not only provides the necessary light stimulation but also engages users in a way that enhances their overall mood and well-being.

Moreover, VR can facilitate personalized therapeutic experiences tailored to individual needs. Through the use of generative AI, these virtual environments can adapt based on user preferences and emotional responses. For instance, a person may benefit from a calming beach scene one day and a vibrant, bustling cityscape the next, depending on their mood. This level of customization ensures that the therapeutic experience remains relevant and effective, thereby increasing user engagement and the likelihood of positive outcomes.

In addition to its therapeutic applications, VR can foster community and social connection among individuals experiencing SAD. By creating shared virtual spaces, users can engage with others facing similar challenges, providing a platform for support and interaction. This communal aspect of VR can help combat the isolation often felt by those with SAD, encouraging users to share experiences and coping strategies in a safe and supportive environment.

Finally, the integration of AI-powered mood tracking apps with VR experiences can enhance the overall treatment of SAD. These applications can monitor users' emotional states and provide real-time feedback, allowing for adjustments to their VR therapy sessions as needed. This synergy between technology and therapeutic practice not only empowers individuals to take charge of their mental health but also promotes a more comprehensive approach to managing SAD. As VR technology continues to evolve, its potential to support individuals in overcoming the challenges of Seasonal Affective Disorder becomes increasingly apparent.

Future Trends in VR Light Therapy

Future trends in VR light therapy are poised to transform how individuals experiencing seasonal affective disorder (SAD) access treatment and support. Advances in technology, particularly within the realms of virtual reality and artificial intelligence, promise to enhance the efficacy and personalization of light therapy. As awareness grows around the impact of SAD, the integration of VR environments with light therapy stands out as a promising solution, allowing users to immerse themselves in settings designed to elevate mood and foster a sense of well-being.

One significant trend is the development of highly customizable VR environments that cater to individual preferences and needs. Users will have the ability to select from a variety of virtual landscapes, such as sunlit beaches or serene woodland settings, which can be combined with tailored light therapy sessions. This personalization can enhance engagement and efficacy, as individuals may respond more positively to environments that resonate with their personal experiences and emotional needs. As technology evolves, these environments will become increasingly sophisticated, utilizing real-time data to adjust lighting and scenery based on user feedback and mood tracking.

Moreover, the integration of AI-powered mood tracking apps will revolutionize the way users interact with VR light therapy. These applications can analyze user behavior and emotional states through biometric data and self-reports, allowing for more precise adjustments in therapy sessions. By leveraging generative AI, mood tracking apps will not only suggest appropriate VR environments but also provide insights into patterns and triggers associated with SAD, empowering users to take a more active role in their treatment. This data-driven approach will facilitate more effective interventions and enhance overall outcomes for individuals dealing with seasonal mood fluctuations.

The emergence of personalized AI therapy chatbots will also play a crucial role in the future of VR light therapy. These chatbots can offer real-time support and guidance, helping users navigate their experiences and providing coping strategies for managing SAD symptoms. By incorporating elements of cognitive behavioral therapy and positive psychology, these virtual assistants can reinforce the benefits of light therapy and encourage users to engage consistently with their treatment plans. This integration of AI chatbots not only enhances accessibility but also ensures that users have an additional layer of support tailored to their unique challenges.

Finally, AI-driven community support platforms are expected to gain traction, fostering awareness and connection among individuals experiencing SAD. These platforms will facilitate the sharing of experiences, tips, and resources, creating a supportive network that reinforces the importance of light therapy and mental health awareness. By harnessing the power of generative AI, these communities can curate relevant content, organize virtual meetups, and promote collective well-being initiatives. As awareness of SAD continues to grow, these platforms will play an essential role in combating stigma and enhancing the overall effectiveness of treatment strategies, ultimately guiding individuals from darkness to light.

Chapter 5: Personalized AI Therapy Chatbots for SAD Support

How AI Chatbots Work in Mental Health

AI chatbots are increasingly becoming integral tools in the mental health sector, particularly for individuals suffering from Seasonal Affective Disorder (SAD). These intelligent systems leverage advanced algorithms and natural language processing to provide timely support and guidance. By simulating human-like conversations, AI chatbots can offer therapeutic interactions that help users navigate their emotional challenges. This is particularly valuable for those experiencing SAD, as the condition often leads to feelings of isolation and despair during the darker months of the year.

The mechanics of AI chatbots in mental health involve a combination of data analysis, user input, and emotional recognition. When users engage with a chatbot, their responses are analyzed to identify patterns in mood and sentiment. This allows the chatbot to tailor its responses and suggestions to meet the individual needs of the user. For instance, if a user expresses feelings of sadness or lethargy, the chatbot can recommend coping strategies, such as engaging in light therapy or participating in outdoor activities that promote exposure to natural light, which is crucial for those affected by SAD.

AI-powered mood tracking apps complement chatbots by allowing users to log their feelings and experiences over time. These applications can analyze mood patterns and provide insights that guide the chatbot's interactions. By integrating mood tracking, the chatbot can become more effective in offering personalized support, as it can refer back to previous entries to provide contextually relevant advice. This ongoing dialogue fosters a sense of connection, enabling users to feel understood and supported throughout their journey with SAD.

Moreover, virtual reality environments can enhance the experience of using AI chatbots for users dealing with SAD. These immersive experiences can simulate exposure to sunlight and nature, helping to mitigate some of the symptoms associated with seasonal depression. Chatbots can serve as guides within these environments, offering encouragement and mindfulness techniques that further enhance the therapeutic experience. This multi-faceted approach allows users to engage with their mental health in a dynamic and interactive manner, promoting a sense of agency and empowerment.

The integration of generative AI into seasonal wellness plans also plays a critical role in supporting individuals with SAD. By analyzing large datasets of successful strategies, AI can generate personalized wellness plans that include activities, dietary recommendations, and social engagement tactics tailored to the user's preferences and lifestyle. Additionally, AI-driven community support platforms can foster connections among individuals experiencing similar challenges, creating a sense of belonging and shared understanding. Through these various applications, AI chatbots emerge as vital resources in the fight against seasonal affective disorder, offering innovative solutions that can adapt to the evolving needs of users.

Effectiveness of Chatbots for SAD Support

The effectiveness of chatbots for supporting individuals with Seasonal Affective Disorder (SAD) has become a focal point in mental health interventions. These AI-powered tools offer immediate, accessible support for the estimated two million people in the UK and twelve million across Northern Europe who experience SAD annually. Chatbots can provide users with a range of functionalities, including mood tracking, symptom assessment, and personalized recommendations, making them a valuable resource for those seeking assistance outside traditional therapy settings.

One of the key advantages of chatbots is their ability to engage users in a non-judgmental, private environment. Individuals with SAD may find it challenging to discuss their feelings with others, leading to feelings of isolation. Chatbots can offer an alternative by creating a safe space for users to express their emotions and receive instant feedback. This immediacy can be particularly beneficial during the darker months when symptoms may intensify, allowing individuals to manage their mood fluctuations proactively.

Moreover, the integration of AI-driven mood tracking apps enhances the effectiveness of chatbots by providing real-time data on users' emotional states. These applications can prompt users to document their feelings and behaviors, enabling the chatbot to tailor its responses and suggestions based on individual patterns. This level of personalization can lead to improved engagement and adherence to self-care strategies, ultimately leading to more effective management of SAD symptoms.

In addition to mood tracking, personalized AI therapy chatbots can deliver cognitive-behavioral techniques and mindfulness exercises specifically designed for individuals with SAD. By incorporating these evidence-based approaches, chatbots can empower users to develop coping strategies that resonate with their unique experiences. This is particularly important as the one-size-fits-all model often fails to address the complexities of mental health challenges, making personalized support crucial for effective intervention.

Lastly, the role of chatbots in fostering community support cannot be overlooked. Through AI-driven platforms, users can connect with others who share similar experiences, creating a sense of belonging and validation. This communal aspect can further enhance the effectiveness of chatbot interventions, as individuals learn from one another and feel less alone in their struggles. As generative AI continues to evolve, the potential for chatbots to provide comprehensive, empathetic support for those affected by SAD will likely expand, contributing significantly to seasonal wellbeing strategies.

User Interaction and Satisfaction

User interaction and satisfaction are critical components in the development and implementation of generative AI tools aimed at addressing Seasonal Affective Disorder (SAD). Given that millions across Europe contend with this condition annually, understanding how users engage with these technologies can significantly influence their effectiveness. Health care providers and mental health professionals must prioritize user experience to ensure that AI-powered applications, virtual reality environments, and personalized therapy chatbots meet the needs of those suffering from SAD. This subchapter explores the various dimensions of user interaction, emphasizing the importance of creating intuitive, accessible, and responsive platforms.

AI-powered mood tracking apps serve as a primary interface for users seeking to monitor their emotional well-being throughout the seasonal fluctuations. These applications must not only collect data effectively but also present it in a manner that users find engaging and easy to understand. Features such as simple user interfaces, clear visualizations of mood patterns, and the ability to set personal goals can enhance user satisfaction. Additionally, incorporating feedback mechanisms can allow users to communicate their experiences, which can inform ongoing improvements in app functionality. Tailoring interactions to user preferences enhances their willingness to engage regularly, fostering a greater commitment to tracking their moods and identifying patterns related to SAD.

Virtual reality environments designed for seasonal light therapy represent another innovative approach to user interaction and satisfaction. These immersive experiences can transport users to sunlit locales, simulating the effects of natural light exposure. To maximize engagement, it is essential that these environments are not only visually appealing but also customizable based on individual preferences. Users should be able to select from various settings, intensity levels, and duration of exposure to ensure that the experience aligns with their needs. Feedback from users can guide enhancements, ensuring that virtual reality tools remain relevant and effective in alleviating symptoms associated with SAD.

Personalized AI therapy chatbots offer a unique opportunity for users to receive immediate support tailored to their specific circumstances. These chatbots should employ natural language processing to facilitate meaningful conversations, making users feel understood and supported. The design of these interactions must prioritize empathy and responsiveness, with the ability to adapt to user emotions in real-time. Regular updates based on user input can enhance the chatbot's effectiveness, ensuring that it evolves to meet the changing needs of individuals experiencing SAD. By fostering a sense of connection and understanding, these AI-driven tools can significantly improve user satisfaction and drive better mental health outcomes.

Lastly, AI-driven community support platforms play a vital role in increasing awareness and providing a space for individuals affected by SAD to connect. These platforms should encourage interaction through forums, resource sharing, and peer support systems. User satisfaction hinges on the ability to find relevant information and connect with others who share similar experiences. Integrating features such as anonymous discussions and moderated groups can create a safe environment for users to share their struggles and successes. By prioritizing user interaction and fostering a sense of community, these platforms can enhance the overall experience for individuals seeking support for SAD, ultimately contributing to their seasonal well-being.

Chapter 6: Generative AI for Creating Seasonal Wellness Plans

The Importance of Personalized Wellness Plans

The importance of personalized wellness plans cannot be overstated, especially in the context of managing Seasonal Affective Disorder (SAD). With approximately 2 million people in the UK and around 12 million across Northern Europe experiencing SAD annually, tailored strategies are essential for effective treatment. Personalized wellness plans take into account an individual's unique circumstances, preferences, and health backgrounds, ensuring that interventions are more relevant and impactful. These plans can leverage generative AI to analyze vast amounts of data, creating customized approaches that cater to specific symptoms and lifestyle factors related to SAD.

Generative AI has the capability to develop individualized wellness plans by integrating mood tracking data and environmental factors. AI-powered mood tracking apps can collect real-time information on an individual's emotional state, sleep patterns, and daily routines. By analyzing this data, generative AI can suggest specific interventions that align with the user's needs. For instance, if a user reports increased feelings of sadness during specific months, the app can recommend a combination of light therapy, exercise, and social activities tailored to those periods. This level of personalization enhances the likelihood of adherence to the wellness plan, as individuals are more likely to engage with strategies that resonate with their personal experiences.

The integration of virtual reality environments for seasonal light therapy represents another innovative approach to personalized wellness plans. These environments can simulate natural sunlight exposure, which is crucial for individuals suffering from SAD. By customizing the intensity and duration of light exposure based on user feedback and preferences, generative AI can create immersive experiences that promote mood elevation. Users can interact with their virtual environments, adjusting settings to find what works best for them. Such personalization not only improves the effectiveness of light therapy but also empowers users to take an active role in their mental health management.

Furthermore, personalized AI therapy chatbots offer another layer of support for those dealing with SAD. These chatbots can engage in conversations that are tailored to the user's emotional state and specific challenges. By utilizing natural language processing and machine learning, chatbots can provide immediate responses, coping strategies, and encouragement based on the user's unique situation. This immediacy and relevance can significantly enhance the therapeutic experience, making users feel more understood and supported during their difficult moments. Chatbots can also track users' progress over time, allowing for continual adjustments to their wellness plans.

Lastly, AI-driven community support platforms play a vital role in raising awareness and fostering connections among those affected by SAD. These platforms can curate resources, share success stories, and facilitate discussions among users who share similar experiences. By analyzing user interactions, generative AI can recommend relevant content and community groups, further personalizing the support experience. This sense of community is crucial for combating feelings of isolation often associated with SAD, as individuals can find solidarity and understanding from others who are navigating similar challenges. Together, these elements underscore the transformative potential of personalized wellness plans in managing Seasonal Affective Disorder and improving overall mental health outcomes.

How Generative AI Can Tailor Wellness Strategies

Generative AI holds significant promise in developing personalized wellness strategies tailored specifically for individuals suffering from Seasonal Affective Disorder (SAD). This condition, which affects around two million people in the UK and approximately 12 million across northern Europe each year, often leads to feelings of depression and lethargy during the winter months when daylight is scarce. By harnessing the capabilities of generative AI, healthcare providers and mental health professionals can create customized interventions that address the unique symptoms and triggers of SAD for each individual, leading to more effective management strategies.

One of the most impactful applications of generative AI in this context is the development of AI-powered mood tracking apps. These applications use algorithms to analyze users' daily emotional states, sleep patterns, and activity levels, helping them identify trends and triggers related to their SAD symptoms. By processing this data, generative AI can generate personalized insights and suggestions to enhance mood and overall well-being. For example, the app might recommend specific light therapy sessions or outdoor activities based on the user's unique mood patterns, fostering a proactive approach to managing their condition.

In addition to mood tracking, virtual reality (VR) environments designed specifically for seasonal light therapy represent another innovative use of generative AI. These immersive experiences can simulate bright, sunny environments, effectively combating the lack of natural light that contributes to SAD. By tailoring the VR experience to individual preferences and responses to light therapy, generative AI can optimize these treatments, making them more enjoyable and effective. Users can engage with these environments in a way that feels personalized, enhancing the therapeutic experience and increasing adherence to treatment plans.

Furthermore, personalized AI therapy chatbots can serve as valuable support tools for individuals facing SAD. These chatbots, powered by generative AI, can engage users in supportive conversations, providing coping strategies and emotional support when traditional therapy may not be readily available. By analyzing user interactions and feedback, these chatbots can adapt their responses over time, ensuring that the support offered aligns with the individual's evolving needs. This creates an accessible and responsive resource for those who may be hesitant to seek help through conventional means.

Lastly, generative AI can facilitate the creation of seasonal wellness plans tailored to individual needs and circumstances. By compiling data on a person's routines, preferences, and specific symptoms of SAD, AI-driven platforms can generate comprehensive wellness strategies that incorporate various interventions, such as exercise, dietary changes, and social activities. Additionally, AI-driven community support platforms can enhance awareness and provide connection opportunities for individuals experiencing SAD. These platforms can foster a sense of community, allowing users to share experiences, strategies, and emotional support while benefiting from the insights of generative AI to create a more informed and supportive network.

Success Stories from Implemented Wellness Plans

Success stories from implemented wellness plans showcase the transformative impact that targeted interventions can have on individuals experiencing Seasonal Affective Disorder (SAD). One such success story involves a community health initiative in the UK that integrated generative AI to create personalized seasonal wellness plans. Participants were provided with AI-generated recommendations tailored to their specific symptoms and preferences. Over a six-month period, feedback from participants indicated a significant reduction in depressive symptoms and an increase in overall well-being. The structured approach of combining AI insights with traditional therapeutic practices enabled many individuals to better manage their seasonal mood fluctuations.

Another notable example comes from the use of AI-powered mood tracking apps specifically designed for those with SAD. One prominent app analyzed user data to identify patterns in mood changes relative to seasonal variations and environmental factors such as sunlight exposure. By offering real-time feedback and personalized suggestions, users were able to implement changes in their daily routines that enhanced their mood and energy levels. Many users reported improved engagement in social activities and a renewed sense of hope as they learned to anticipate and manage their symptoms proactively.

Virtual reality environments have also emerged as a powerful tool in the fight against SAD. One innovative study utilized immersive light therapy sessions through VR technology, allowing participants to experience bright, sunny environments regardless of the weather outside. Participants reported feeling uplifted after just a few sessions, with many noting a significant decrease in feelings of lethargy and isolation. This approach not only provided immediate relief but also fostered a sense of connection to brighter, warmer experiences that many missed during the darker months of the year.

The implementation of personalized AI therapy chatbots has transformed access to mental health support for those suffering from SAD. One healthcare provider integrated an AI chatbot that offered 24/7 support, providing users with coping strategies and encouragement tailored to their specific situations. Users found the chatbot to be a non-judgmental source of support, which significantly improved their willingness to seek help. Many reported a reduction in feelings of loneliness and an increase in their ability to cope with seasonal challenges, highlighting the effectiveness of blending technology with mental health care.

Lastly, AI-driven community support platforms have played a crucial role in raising awareness and fostering connections among individuals affected by SAD. One platform successfully organized virtual meetups where members could share their experiences and coping strategies, facilitated by AI tools that matched users based on similarities in their experiences. This sense of community not only provided emotional support but also encouraged participants to adopt healthier habits, resulting in improved mental health outcomes overall. These success stories illustrate the potential of generative AI and innovative wellness strategies to create meaningful change for those facing the challenges of Seasonal Affective Disorder.

Chapter 7: AI-Driven Community Support Platforms for SAD Awareness

Building Online Communities for SAD Support

Building an online community for Seasonal Affective Disorder (SAD) support offers a powerful avenue for individuals to connect, share experiences, and access resources. Given that millions of people across the UK and Northern Europe face the challenges of SAD each year, fostering a supportive online environment can significantly improve well-being. Online communities can provide a safe space where individuals can discuss their struggles, share coping strategies, and receive encouragement from those who truly understand their experiences. Leveraging technology, these platforms can enhance the reach and effectiveness of support, enabling participants to find solace and camaraderie in a collective journey toward improved mental health.

Generative AI can play a transformative role in creating and sustaining these online communities. By utilizing AI-driven tools, community managers can tailor content and resources to meet the specific needs of their members. For instance, AI algorithms can analyze engagement patterns and identify common concerns among participants, which can inform the creation of relevant discussion topics and resource sharing. This customization not only fosters a sense of belonging but also encourages active participation, as members see their needs being addressed in real-time. Furthermore, personalized feedback from AI can guide users toward appropriate resources, whether that be articles, videos, or relevant community discussions.

AI-powered mood tracking apps can also be integrated into these online communities, offering members a way to monitor their emotional states over time. Through regular check-ins and data analysis, users can gain insights into their mood patterns and identify triggers related to SAD. This data can then be shared within the community, allowing for constructive conversations and collective support. By understanding how SAD affects their emotional landscape, individuals can better articulate their needs and seek assistance, ultimately fostering a more robust support network.

Virtual reality environments present another innovative approach to building online SAD support communities. These immersive platforms can simulate sunlight exposure, providing a therapeutic experience that can alleviate some symptoms of SAD. By incorporating virtual reality into community activities, members can engage in group light therapy sessions, participate in shared experiences, and even explore virtual environments designed to uplift mood. This technology not only enhances the therapeutic aspects of community gatherings but also offers an exciting and interactive way for individuals to connect and support one another.

Finally, personalized AI therapy chatbots can serve as immediate resources for community members seeking help. These chatbots can offer instant support, guiding users through coping strategies, mindfulness exercises, and self-care tips tailored to their individual circumstances. By providing 24/7 access to mental health resources, chatbots can bridge the gap between professional help and community support, ensuring that individuals have a reliable outlet for their concerns. Additionally, as these chatbots learn from user interactions, they can continually improve their responses, making them increasingly effective in addressing the unique challenges faced by those with SAD. This integration of AI technologies not only enhances community engagement but also empowers individuals to take proactive steps toward managing their mental health.

Tools and Features of Community Platforms

Community platforms have emerged as vital tools in supporting individuals coping with Seasonal Affective Disorder (SAD), particularly through the integration of generative AI technologies. These platforms provide a space for individuals to connect, share experiences, and access resources tailored to their unique needs. By leveraging the power of AI, these tools enhance engagement and foster a sense of community among users who may feel isolated due to their seasonal mood fluctuations.

One of the most significant features of these community platforms is AI-powered mood tracking apps. These applications allow users to log their daily emotional states and identify patterns related to their mood changes throughout the seasons. By analyzing this data, the apps can offer personalized insights, helping users recognize triggers and develop coping strategies. This feature not only empowers individuals to take control of their mental health but also facilitates communication with healthcare providers who can use this data to inform treatment plans.

Virtual reality environments are another innovative tool offered by community platforms that cater to those experiencing SAD. These immersive experiences simulate exposure to natural light, which is often lacking during the darker months. Users can engage with these virtual environments from the comfort of their homes, providing a therapeutic escape that can enhance mood and alleviate symptoms. Moreover, these VR sessions can be integrated into community activities, encouraging users to participate together and share their experiences, thereby strengthening the support network.

Personalized AI therapy chatbots have also become essential components of community platforms. These chatbots provide immediate support and guidance, offering users a safe space to express their feelings and receive tailored responses. The AI can suggest coping mechanisms, mindfulness exercises, or direct users to relevant resources within the community. This feature ensures that help is always accessible, reducing the stigma associated with seeking mental health support and promoting a proactive approach to managing SAD.

Lastly, generative AI plays a crucial role in creating seasonal wellness plans tailored to individual needs. By analyzing user data and preferences, AI can generate personalized strategies that encompass physical, emotional, and social well-being. These plans may include recommendations for light therapy, physical activity, and social engagement, all aimed at mitigating the effects of SAD. Coupled with AI-driven community support, these features encourage collective awareness and understanding of SAD, fostering a more informed and compassionate environment for individuals navigating their mental health challenges.

The Impact of Community Support on Mental Health

The role of community support in enhancing mental health, particularly for those affected by Seasonal Affective Disorder (SAD), is increasingly recognized as a vital component of effective treatment strategies. Research indicates that social connectedness can significantly alleviate feelings of isolation and despair commonly experienced during the winter months. Community support provides individuals with a network of understanding peers, fostering environments where shared experiences can lead to collective coping strategies. This communal approach not only reinforces a sense of belonging but also empowers individuals to seek help and share their struggles openly.

Generative AI technologies are revolutionizing the way community support is structured and delivered, particularly for individuals grappling with SAD. AI-powered mood tracking apps can facilitate interaction among users, allowing them to share their daily emotional states and experiences. This data-driven approach enhances group dynamics, as individuals can identify patterns and triggers that affect their mood during the changing seasons. Furthermore, these apps can encourage users to engage with one another, creating a supportive online environment that mirrors the benefits of traditional community support systems.

Virtual reality environments are another innovative tool being employed to combat the effects of SAD. These immersive experiences can simulate natural light exposure and create virtual spaces where users can interact with others in a supportive setting. By combining the therapeutic benefits of light therapy with community engagement, individuals can experience improved mood and mental health outcomes. This approach not only addresses the physiological aspects of SAD but also fosters social interaction, which is equally important for mental wellbeing.

Personalized AI therapy chatbots have emerged as an essential resource for those seeking immediate support. These chatbots can provide real-time assistance and guidance tailored to individual needs, allowing users to access help whenever they need it. By integrating community support features, such as connecting users with local support groups or online forums, these chatbots can enhance the overall therapeutic experience. This fusion of personalized care and community engagement can lead to more effective coping mechanisms and improved mental health outcomes for individuals dealing with SAD.

Lastly, AI-driven community support platforms play a crucial role in raising awareness about SAD and its impacts. By leveraging data analytics and community feedback, these platforms can identify gaps in support services and promote initiatives that encourage collective action. This not only enhances public understanding of SAD but also mobilizes resources and volunteers within communities to provide support. As awareness grows, so does the potential for individuals to find solace and strength in shared experiences, ultimately paving the way for a brighter collective future for those affected by Seasonal Affective Disorder.

Chapter 8: Integrating Generative AI in Traditional Mental Health Practices

Collaboration Between AI Tools and Mental Health Professionals

Collaboration between AI tools and mental health professionals represents a transformative approach to addressing Seasonal Affective Disorder (SAD), particularly in regions where the condition is prevalent. With approximately two million individuals in the UK and twelve million across northern Europe affected by SAD annually, the integration of advanced AI technologies into mental health care can enhance the effectiveness of traditional therapeutic methods. Mental health professionals can leverage AI-powered mood tracking apps to monitor patients' emotional states, identify patterns, and provide timely interventions. By utilizing data analytics, therapists can gain insights into the seasonal fluctuations in their clients' moods, allowing for a tailored treatment approach that addresses individual needs.

AI-powered mood tracking apps serve as valuable tools for both patients and practitioners. These applications allow users to record their feelings and behaviors in real time, creating a comprehensive profile of their emotional well-being. Health care providers can analyze this data to discern trends, enabling them to adapt treatment plans based on real-time feedback. Furthermore, these apps can send reminders for self-care activities and mood check-ins, fostering proactive engagement from patients. This collaboration ensures that mental health professionals are not working in isolation but are supported by data-driven insights that can enhance therapeutic outcomes.

Virtual reality environments also play a significant role in the collaboration between AI and mental health professionals. These immersive platforms can simulate natural light exposure, which is particularly beneficial for individuals suffering from SAD who may experience a lack of sunlight during the winter months. When combined with the expertise of mental health professionals, virtual reality can be used as an adjunct to traditional therapies, allowing patients to experience the therapeutic benefits of light exposure in a controlled and engaging setting. This innovative approach not only enhances the treatment experience but also provides professionals with a novel tool to address the specific needs of their patients.

Personalized AI therapy chatbots are another remarkable development in the collaboration between technology and mental health care. These chatbots can offer immediate support and coping strategies to individuals experiencing symptoms of SAD, making mental health resources more accessible. By utilizing natural language processing and machine learning, these chatbots can engage in meaningful conversations, providing users with a sense of companionship and guidance. Mental health professionals can oversee these interactions, ensuring that the responses align with therapeutic goals and offer appropriate support. This synergy enhances the overall care experience while reducing the burden on mental health services.

Finally, AI-driven community support platforms are essential for raising awareness and fostering a sense of belonging among individuals affected by SAD. These platforms can connect users with others who share similar experiences, promoting peer support and community engagement. Mental health professionals can collaborate with these platforms to facilitate discussions, share resources, and provide expert insights. By harnessing the power of generative AI, these platforms can create personalized seasonal wellness plans that incorporate user input, expert recommendations, and evidence-based strategies. This holistic approach not only empowers patients but also creates a supportive environment that encourages recovery and resilience in the face of seasonal challenges.

Training and Education for Healthcare Providers

Training and education for healthcare providers are critical components in effectively addressing Seasonal Affective Disorder (SAD) using generative AI technologies. With millions affected by SAD, especially in northern Europe, healthcare professionals must be equipped with the knowledge and skills to leverage AI-driven solutions. This involves understanding the nature of SAD, its symptoms, and the potential of innovative technologies to enhance patient care. Providers must be trained to recognize the signs of SAD and differentiate it from other mood disorders, ensuring that they can offer appropriate interventions and support.

Incorporating AI-powered mood tracking apps into clinical practice requires healthcare providers to receive training on the functionality and application of these tools. These apps allow individuals to monitor their mood fluctuations and identify patterns related to seasonal changes. By understanding how to interpret the data generated by these apps, healthcare providers can tailor interventions more effectively. Education programs should emphasize the importance of integrating patient feedback and mood tracking data into treatment plans, fostering a collaborative approach between providers and patients.

Virtual reality (VR) environments offer a novel method for seasonal light therapy, and healthcare providers need to be familiar with these technologies to effectively incorporate them into treatment protocols. Training should cover the science behind VR therapy, its benefits for patients with SAD, and best practices for implementation. Providers should also be educated on the various VR options available, ensuring they can advise patients on suitable choices that align with their preferences and comfort levels. This understanding can enhance patient engagement and adherence to treatment, ultimately improving outcomes.

Personalized AI therapy chatbots represent another innovative approach to managing SAD, providing patients with immediate support and guidance. Healthcare providers should be trained to understand how these chatbots function, their limitations, and how they can be effectively integrated into traditional therapeutic practices. This training should include strategies for recommending chatbot use to patients and maintaining an open line of communication to discuss their experiences and concerns. By fostering a collaborative relationship with technology, providers can enhance the overall therapeutic process.

Finally, education on AI-driven community support platforms for SAD awareness is essential for healthcare providers. These platforms can facilitate connections among individuals experiencing similar challenges, creating a sense of community and reducing feelings of isolation. Training should focus on how to utilize these platforms to promote awareness, share resources, and encourage patient participation in support groups. Providers can play a pivotal role in guiding patients toward these resources, thereby enhancing both individual and collective strategies for managing SAD. Through comprehensive training and education, healthcare providers can become effective advocates for innovative solutions that significantly improve the lives of those affected by Seasonal Affective Disorder.

Future Directions for AI in Mental Health

The future of artificial intelligence in mental health, particularly in addressing Seasonal Affective Disorder (SAD), holds significant promise. With approximately 2 million people in the UK and 12 million across northern Europe suffering from SAD annually, the need for innovative approaches to treatment and support is critical. AI technologies are poised to enhance existing methods and introduce new solutions that can alleviate the burden of this condition. By harnessing the capabilities of generative AI, mental health practitioners can create tailored interventions that cater to the unique needs of individuals experiencing seasonal mood fluctuations.

AI-powered mood tracking applications are emerging as valuable tools for individuals managing SAD. These apps can utilize machine learning algorithms to analyze user data and identify patterns in mood changes relative to seasonal changes. This real-time tracking allows users to become more aware of their emotional states and triggers, fostering proactive management strategies. Future advancements may see these applications integrating with wearable technology to provide even more personalized insights, enabling users to receive timely interventions or suggestions for coping strategies based on their specific data.

Virtual reality (VR) environments represent another exciting frontier in the treatment of SAD. These immersive experiences can simulate natural light exposure, which is often limited during the darker months. By creating realistic and engaging virtual settings that mimic outdoor experiences, individuals can experience therapeutic benefits without needing to travel. Future developments in VR technology may lead to customizable environments tailored to individual preferences, further enhancing the effectiveness of light therapy for those suffering from seasonal mood disorders.

Personalized AI therapy chatbots offer an innovative approach to providing immediate support for individuals with SAD. These chatbots can be programmed to deliver cognitive-behavioral therapy techniques, offer coping strategies, and serve as a point of connection when professional help is not immediately available. As AI continues to evolve, these chatbots may incorporate more advanced natural language processing capabilities, allowing for even more nuanced and empathetic interactions. This could help bridge the gap in mental health support, especially for individuals who may be hesitant to seek traditional therapy.

Finally, AI-driven community support platforms can play a pivotal role in raising awareness and fostering connections among individuals affected by SAD. These platforms can facilitate peer support groups, share educational resources, and promote community events focused on mental health. Generative AI can assist in creating seasonal wellness plans tailored to the unique challenges posed by SAD, providing users with actionable strategies to improve their mental wellbeing. In the future, these platforms may leverage data analytics to identify trends and needs within communities, ensuring that resources are allocated effectively to support those most in need.

Chapter 9: Challenges and Limitations of AI in Addressing SAD

Technical Limitations of AI Solutions

The integration of artificial intelligence into healthcare, particularly for conditions like Seasonal Affective Disorder (SAD), presents a range of innovative solutions. However, it is essential to acknowledge the technical limitations that accompany these advancements. Understanding these limitations is crucial for healthcare providers, mental health professionals, and public health advocates as they navigate the potential and challenges of AI applications in seasonal wellbeing strategies.

One significant limitation is the dependency on data quality and availability. AI systems, including mood tracking apps and personalized therapy chatbots, rely on large datasets to make informed predictions and recommendations. In the context of SAD, the lack of comprehensive and high-quality data can hinder the effectiveness of these AI solutions. Many users may not consistently record their moods or engage with the applications, leading to gaps in data that can skew results and limit the accuracy of AI-driven insights. Furthermore, privacy concerns may deter individuals from sharing sensitive information, which is critical for developing effective AI algorithms.

Another challenge lies in the variability of individual responses to treatment. Generative AI technologies, such as virtual reality environments for light therapy and personalized wellness plans, may not account for the diverse experiences of those suffering from SAD. Factors such as genetics, lifestyle, and co-existing mental health conditions can influence how individuals respond to AI-generated interventions. As a result, the one-size-fits-all approach often seen in AI applications may not adequately cater to the nuanced needs of every patient, potentially leading to suboptimal outcomes.

Moreover, there is the issue of technological accessibility and digital literacy. While AI-powered solutions hold the promise of enhancing support for those affected by SAD, not all potential users may have the necessary resources or skills to utilize these technologies effectively. Individuals with limited access to smartphones or the internet, as well as those who lack familiarity with digital platforms, may find themselves excluded from AI-driven support systems. This digital divide can exacerbate existing inequalities in mental health care, particularly for marginalized communities who are already disproportionately affected by SAD.

Finally, the ethical implications of AI in mental health care cannot be overlooked. The reliance on algorithms to guide treatment decisions raises concerns about accountability and transparency. In the case of AI-driven community support platforms for SAD awareness, it is essential to ensure that the information provided is not only accurate but also sensitive to the needs of those seeking help. The potential for bias in AI systems, stemming from the data they are trained on, can lead to the reinforcement of harmful stereotypes or the marginalization of certain groups. Therefore, it is vital for stakeholders in health care and public health to critically assess the ethical dimensions of AI solutions and work towards creating equitable and inclusive frameworks.

In conclusion, while AI offers promising avenues for addressing Seasonal Affective Disorder, it is imperative to recognize and address the technical limitations inherent in these systems. By fostering an informed dialogue among healthcare providers, mental health professionals, and public health advocates, the aim should be to enhance the efficacy of AI solutions while ensuring they are accessible, ethical, and tailored to the diverse needs of individuals experiencing SAD.

Societal and Cultural Barriers

Societal and cultural barriers significantly impact the understanding and treatment of Seasonal Affective Disorder (SAD), particularly in regions where it affects millions annually. In the UK and across northern Europe, the prevalence of SAD often goes unrecognized or misunderstood, leading to stigma around mental health issues. This stigma can prevent individuals from seeking help or discussing their experiences, perpetuating feelings of isolation. Societal perceptions of mental health can create an environment where those suffering from SAD may feel compelled to hide their symptoms, resulting in a lack of awareness about the disorder's impact on daily life.

Cultural attitudes toward mental health also play a crucial role in how SAD is perceived and managed. In some cultures, mental health issues are viewed as a personal weakness, making individuals hesitant to acknowledge their struggles. This cultural backdrop can discourage open discussions about seasonal depression, leading to misinformation and a lack of community support. Additionally, traditional views on mental health treatment may not align with innovative solutions, such as generative AI technologies, which could provide effective support for those affected by SAD. Bridging this cultural gap is essential for fostering acceptance and encouraging individuals to seek appropriate care.

The integration of technology into mental health care presents both opportunities and challenges in addressing societal barriers. AI-powered mood tracking apps, for instance, can facilitate self-awareness and encourage users to recognize patterns in their emotional states. However, for these tools to be effective, they must overcome skepticism surrounding their efficacy. Individuals may question the validity of digital interventions, which are often perceived as impersonal compared to traditional face-to-face therapy. Therefore, it is vital to create educational campaigns that inform the public about the benefits and limitations of AI-driven solutions for managing SAD.

Moreover, the implementation of virtual reality environments for seasonal light therapy can be hindered by societal misconceptions regarding technology's role in mental health care. While these immersive experiences offer promising avenues for treatment, they may be dismissed by those who are unfamiliar with or distrustful of technological advancements. It is crucial to highlight success stories and research findings that showcase the potential of these innovative approaches to build confidence among the public and healthcare providers. Cultivating a culture that embraces technology as a complement to traditional practices can enhance the effectiveness of these interventions.

Finally, community support platforms powered by generative AI can play a pivotal role in breaking down barriers related to SAD. These platforms can foster connections among individuals facing similar challenges, creating a sense of belonging and shared experience. By promoting awareness and understanding, these initiatives can help normalize discussions around SAD and encourage proactive engagement with mental health resources. Ultimately, addressing societal and cultural barriers is essential for ensuring that individuals affected by SAD receive the support they need, leveraging the potential of generative AI to transform seasonal wellbeing strategies.

Addressing Misinformation and Stigma

Addressing misinformation about Seasonal Affective Disorder (SAD) is essential for promoting effective treatment and support systems. Many individuals are unaware of the clinical nature of SAD, often dismissing it as a mere case of "the winter blues." This misunderstanding can lead to stigmatization, where those experiencing SAD feel reluctant to seek help due to the fear of being perceived as weak or overly emotional. By using generative AI technologies, healthcare and mental health professionals can disseminate accurate information about SAD, emphasizing its biological and psychological underpinnings. This proactive approach not only educates the public but also normalizes discussions around mental health, encouraging individuals to seek the assistance they need.

In conjunction with combating misinformation, addressing stigma associated with SAD is equally critical. Stigmatization can exacerbate feelings of isolation and despair among those affected, preventing them from reaching out for support. AI-powered mood tracking apps can play a pivotal role in this regard by fostering a sense of community among users. These platforms can create anonymous spaces where individuals can share their experiences, coping strategies, and symptoms without the fear of judgment. By facilitating peer support and understanding, these tools can help dismantle the stigma surrounding SAD and empower individuals to acknowledge their struggles openly.

Virtual reality environments present another innovative solution for addressing both misinformation and stigma. These environments can simulate natural light exposure, providing users with immersive experiences that can alleviate SAD symptoms. By integrating educational content within these virtual experiences, users can learn about the physiological effects of light on mood regulation while engaging in therapeutic activities. This dual approach not only enhances the effectiveness of seasonal light therapy but also serves to inform users about the realities of SAD, thereby reducing misconceptions and fostering a more supportive community.

Personalized AI therapy chatbots also represent a significant advancement in tackling misinformation and stigma surrounding SAD. These chatbots can provide tailored advice and support based on individual user profiles, ensuring that the information shared is relevant and relatable. By offering immediate access to mental health resources, these AI-driven solutions can help individuals feel less alone in their experiences. Moreover, they can dispel myths by presenting evidence-based information regarding SAD, thus empowering users to understand their condition better and advocate for themselves in seeking appropriate care.

Lastly, AI-driven community support platforms can enhance awareness and understanding of SAD at a societal level. By aggregating data and insights from users, these platforms can identify trends, common misconceptions, and areas needing further education. They can facilitate campaigns aimed at raising awareness about SAD, encouraging community discussions, and promoting local resources. As society becomes more informed about seasonal affective disorder, the stigma surrounding it is likely to diminish, paving the way for more individuals to seek help and engage in strategies that promote their seasonal wellbeing.

Chapter 10: Conclusion and Future Perspectives

Summary of Key Insights

The intersection of generative AI and seasonal wellbeing strategies provides a comprehensive approach to addressing Seasonal Affective Disorder (SAD), particularly relevant to the two million individuals in the UK and twelve million across northern Europe who grapple with this condition each year. The insights presented in this subchapter highlight the transformative potential of technology in enhancing mental health outcomes for those affected by seasonal mood fluctuations. By leveraging generative AI, we can create tailored solutions that not only facilitate recognition and management of SAD but also foster a supportive community environment.

AI-powered mood tracking applications represent a foundational tool in the proactive monitoring of emotional well-being. These apps utilize machine learning algorithms to analyze user data, enabling individuals to identify patterns linked to their mood changes throughout the seasons. By providing real-time feedback, these applications empower users to engage in self-reflection and make informed decisions about their mental health. Moreover, they can facilitate early intervention by alerting users and healthcare providers to significant mood shifts, thereby promoting timely therapeutic responses.

Virtual reality environments have emerged as a groundbreaking method for delivering seasonal light therapy, an essential treatment for SAD. By simulating bright, sunny environments, these VR experiences can effectively mitigate the effects of seasonal darkness, enhancing mood and overall psychological resilience. This immersive approach not only provides immediate relief but also offers a novel means of therapy that can be accessed from the comfort of one's home. The integration of sensory engagement through VR fosters an innovative therapeutic avenue that complements traditional light therapy methods.

Personalized AI therapy chatbots are another promising development in the realm of mental health support for individuals with SAD. These chatbots utilize natural language processing to provide users with tailored conversational therapy, offering emotional support and coping strategies throughout the seasonal cycle. By maintaining availability and anonymity, these AI-driven solutions can reduce barriers to accessing mental health resources, ensuring that individuals feel supported and understood during challenging times. The adaptability of these chatbots allows them to evolve with the user's needs, further enhancing their effectiveness.

Lastly, AI-driven community support platforms play a crucial role in raising awareness and fostering connections among individuals affected by SAD. These platforms leverage generative AI to create engaging content, facilitate peer support networks, and distribute educational resources. By cultivating a sense of community, these platforms not only enhance individuals' understanding of SAD but also reduce feelings of isolation, which can exacerbate the condition. Overall, the integration of generative AI in seasonal wellbeing strategies offers promising insights into the future of mental health care, providing innovative solutions that are both effective and accessible for those navigating the complexities of SAD.

The Future of AI in Seasonal Wellbeing

The future of artificial intelligence in addressing seasonal wellbeing, particularly in relation to Seasonal Affective Disorder (SAD), holds significant promise as technology continues to evolve. With approximately 2 million individuals in the UK and around 12 million across northern Europe affected by SAD annually, the integration of AI into mental health strategies offers innovative solutions. AI-powered mood tracking applications are poised to become crucial tools for individuals experiencing seasonal mood fluctuations. By utilizing machine learning algorithms, these apps can analyze user data to identify patterns and triggers, allowing for timely interventions that can mitigate the severity of depressive episodes associated with changing seasons.

Virtual reality environments designed for seasonal light therapy represent another exciting frontier in the application of AI for mental wellbeing. These immersive experiences can replicate the effects of natural sunlight exposure, which is often lacking during the darker months. By leveraging AI to customize these environments based on individual preferences and responses, users can engage in therapeutic experiences that enhance mood and promote relaxation. This personalized approach not only addresses the symptoms of SAD but also empowers individuals to take an active role in their mental health management.

Personalized AI therapy chatbots are also emerging as a valuable resource for those dealing with SAD. These chatbots can provide real-time emotional support and guidance, helping users navigate their feelings and challenges related to seasonal changes. Equipped with natural language processing capabilities, these AI companions can offer empathy and understanding, facilitating conversations that might be difficult for individuals to have with friends or family. As these technologies advance, they are likely to become increasingly sophisticated, offering tailored interventions and strategies based on user interactions.

Generative AI is poised to play a transformative role in creating seasonal wellness plans tailored to individual needs. By analyzing a person's history, preferences, and specific symptoms, generative AI can suggest a variety of activities, therapies, and lifestyle adjustments that promote wellbeing throughout the year. These personalized wellness plans can include recommendations for physical activity, dietary changes, and mindfulness practices, ensuring that individuals have a comprehensive strategy to combat the effects of SAD. This level of customization enhances the likelihood of adherence and success in managing symptoms.

AI-driven community support platforms are critical for raising awareness and fostering connections among those affected by SAD. These platforms can facilitate discussions, share resources, and promote events focused on seasonal wellbeing. By utilizing AI to moderate and personalize content, these communities can ensure that users engage with relevant information and support networks tailored to their unique experiences. The ability to connect with others who share similar challenges can significantly alleviate feelings of isolation and provide essential encouragement during difficult times. As we look to the future, the intersection of AI and seasonal wellbeing presents a hopeful pathway for improving the mental health landscape for millions affected by SAD.

Call to Action for Stakeholders in Mental Health Care

In addressing the pressing issue of Seasonal Affective Disorder (SAD), a call to action for stakeholders in mental health care is essential to harness the potential of generative AI technologies. The impact of SAD on approximately two million individuals in the UK and twelve million across northern Europe underscores the urgency of developing innovative solutions. Stakeholders, including healthcare providers, mental health organizations, and policymakers, must collaborate to create an integrated approach that leverages generative AI to enhance diagnosis, treatment, and community support for those affected by this seasonal condition.

AI-powered mood tracking apps represent a pivotal tool in the proactive management of SAD. By utilizing machine learning algorithms, these applications can analyze user data to identify patterns in mood fluctuations related to seasonal changes. Stakeholders should prioritize the development and dissemination of these apps to empower individuals with insights into their emotional well-being. This approach not only promotes self-awareness but also encourages users to seek timely interventions when necessary. Mental health professionals can play a crucial role by integrating these tools into their practice, thereby improving patient outcomes through personalized care.

Virtual reality environments offer another innovative solution for light therapy, addressing the core symptoms of SAD. By creating immersive experiences that simulate natural sunlight exposure, these environments can provide therapeutic benefits to users who may be unable to access traditional light therapy. Stakeholders in mental health care should invest in research and development of VR technologies that can be used in clinical settings or at home. Collaboration with tech companies to design user-friendly and accessible platforms will be vital in making this treatment option widely available to those suffering from seasonal mood disorders.

The introduction of personalized AI therapy chatbots can revolutionize support mechanisms for individuals with SAD. These chatbots, powered by generative AI, can deliver tailored responses and coping strategies based on user interactions and emotional states. Stakeholders need to recognize the value of integrating such technologies into mental health care systems, providing users with immediate access to support and resources. Training mental health professionals to work alongside these AI tools can enhance their therapeutic effectiveness, ensuring that individuals receive comprehensive care that combines human empathy with technological advancements.

Lastly, AI-driven community support platforms can foster greater awareness and understanding of SAD within society. By connecting individuals with shared experiences, these platforms can cultivate a supportive network that encourages open discussions about mental health. Stakeholders should advocate for the establishment of these platforms, which can facilitate educational campaigns, peer support groups, and resource sharing. By promoting community engagement and reducing stigma, stakeholders can significantly contribute to a more informed and compassionate approach to seasonal mental health challenges, ultimately leading to improved outcomes for those affected by SAD.

www.ingramcontent.com/pod-product-compliance
Lightning Source LLC
Chambersburg PA
CBHW070419230526
45471CB00006B/2881